**Feet**

**To Water**

Copyright©Holly Elizabeth Dunlap, 2015

Copyright Design and Cover Art©Tiffany Dunlap, 2015

Printed in the United States of America

All Rights Reserved

Library of Congress Control Number: 2015942468

ISBN: 978-0-9857703-7-2

*Feet to Water* by Holly Elizabeth Dunlap

Published by Summerfield Publishing
New Plains Press
Auburn, AL 36831-1946
newplainspress.com

Acknowledgements

"Needmore Road," previously published in BlazeVox, Fall 2013.

"Raw Honey," previously published in Asphalt Sky, (2009).

"Cold Cut Generation," previously published in BlazeVox, Fall 2013 under the title "One House"

for Israel Elizabeth,
my light

**Also, In Grateful Acknowledgement To**

Izzy, you are our sweet and precious gift from God, and I love you more than all the stars in the sky, wider than the ocean, and deeper than the sea! You have an insight and beauty that is boundless and far-reaching, and you are the reason I am here to write these poems.

Mom, I definitely inherited my love of words from you, and you have been my strongest supporter from my first breath to my first tattoo, to my degrees in English and now my adventures in motherhood, and I am so thankful for you.

Tiff, we are so different, but we have an unbreakable bond in sisterhood, creativity, the outdoors, and in teasing one another. Thank you for designing the cover. I am very grateful and thrilled to have your mark on this book!

Dad, you have always been my sweet Daddy who has been for me and with me even when you didn't understand my choices. You inspire me with your dedication to your children, and your silly sense of humor, and I miss our daddy-daughter talks. Much of this book is written because of you. You are such a beautiful soul, even as your body and mind leave us slowly.

Drew, you will always be my sweet little brother, and I am truly blessed to have you. I'm so glad for your intelligence and your fortitude through so many challenges in our lives, and I loved riding (and falling!) down mountains with you. I love you, the man that you are, and you are an inspiration to me.

Becca M., thank you for your pure, steadfast and tenacious friendship, and for sharing your creative fruit with me, and letting me share mine with you! I know no one who could have written my bio like you.

Anna B., you gave us the most beautiful baby shower, and helped so much with the ordering of these poems. You are a truly priceless friend.

John Summerfield, of New Plains Press for believing in my work and making this happen.

Also, thank you kindly to Abraham Smith and Deidre DeLaughter for the lovely blurbs.

To my church family and all of my other amazing friends: I am so grateful to have you all in my life.

# Table of Contents

## Chapter I: When the Dog Barks

When the dog barks [...]makes me think of you  17
One Year  18
Human  19
You know the ashes  20
Tree Hearts  21
Louisiana Sky  22
Daddy  23
Windows  24
Aqua/Terra  25
Nothing But Peeling (or, addict)  26
Still Here  27
Needmore Road  28
We Could  29
The heart  30
on your birthday  31
speaking of swallowing my heart  33
Omen  34

## Chapter II: Feet to Water

Raw Honey  37
a 27  38
Stale Stick  39
late  40
on a full moon  41
fruit  42
Taxonomy (or the history of Christianity)  43
Roundhouse  44
Kiss My Grits  45
Don't Make Me Do It  46
love song for lovers who can't be in love  47
bound, or I feel like a horny Emily Dickinson  48

**Chapter III: The Art of Dreaming**

the art of dreaming  53
Immortals  55
You'll recognize me  56
Scarecrow  57
There's something wrong with me  58
When we run  59
July 4$^{th}$  60
Playing at Religion  61
Shadow, Our Puppet  62
Ripping  63
first day  65
Cold Cut Generation  66
Pollination  67
my bowl  68
to build death  69
Prayer Room Floor  70
Morning Star  71

Author Biography  73

## Chapter 1: When the Dog Barks

**When the dog barks in her sleep, it makes me think of you.**

She makes a low, quiet, muffled sound, like when I punch my pillow, and I won't divide anymore.

I'll cough up this painful pill, wade soggy fields, and laugh alone

on this cold wet ground.

No more wet towels—no more you, heavy on me.

I will fall in light, roll around in my own mouth.

I won't have to look at you when I brush my morning teeth, and I won't whisper your name at night.

Only my own.

**One Year**

after you died,
a storm

climbing the walls outside hissing, bearing
down, cutting sky

filling holes in dirt.

And me, looking for hair clips in the fridge
I very well could have put there.

**Human**

standing outside the funeral home, a man in the parking lot looks at the sky, woman digs in her purse, boys in suits chase one another down sidewalks, a man hugs a woman, rigid faces, some discussing nothing, weather—others maybe.

The way of death is still, sameness, no one doing much different. Like after you were autopsied and incinerated at 38, the eulogist, a stranger, spoke only of your job—

and your father didn't speak of you at all.

There are huge concrete planters

with flowers that will only last a season,

apples that will never be eaten,

rotted under limbs,

bursts of fireworks,

litter from 4th of Julys passed.

**You know the ashes**

of a loved one

contain pieces of bone— obvious

chunks

of bone.

I remember you tasted your brother's —

His ashes didn't change anything

but they must have tasted good — must

have felt like home.

**Tree Hearts**

Don't collect the fallen branches.
I sail this land.
It slowly floats me.
My roots darken in rain.
I reach clouds with my leaves, and
my veins need moisture.


Hearts in my trunk,
a new one each year.
I need multiple hearts
to survive this world.


How much have I spent in your name?
Every day I find new soil
and eat your words so
God won't see them.
I can't imagine how horrible you must feel
spitting shameful faces.


I don't want to lose you.
I want you to see again, but I can't reach that far in.
I can only reach out and up and down.


You need clouds to soften your faces.
You need jade plants
and the soft ash of fallen children to mend your lesions.

## Louisiana Sky

In Louisiana
graves lie above ground,
and cousin,
bones and hair of a 22-year-old,
lies in his casket.

After his death
the sister became bones, too,
parents so blown away
by her brother's death,
a kite lodged in a tree,
they hardly noticed
as she rose, a paper doll,
into white,

where staccato clouds
dot the sky with anger.

**Daddy,**

I hold your hand, driving you home from day care.  I talk.  Just words. Only yes and no questions.

Usually "uh-huh" or "unh-unh" for answers.                I talk about my daughter, the one you can't remember.

I ask, "Did you find it hard to watch us make mistakes growing up?"  Too long a question maybe?

Your eyes scan the scenery.  Maybe you can't hear me, you're distracted, you don't know who I am.

The gap between brain and body, thought and action, thought and thought, gets

wider every day,

and I miss you.

**Windows**

for Becca

We've been looking out of them.
Our faces with small shards—
We are laughing,
Can't stop drawing.
Everything a naked woman.

Laughing in us came from the breaking.

## Aqua/Terra

I lived in the sea before land pushed me toward sky. This is the marriage year. As tectonic plates shift below us, those broken plates change our broken-ness, and I am bathing, cleansing dirt that washes me. Recent ink of pen or berry stains my rock,
like blood stains, menstruation of earth.

This is the year of the parting. Pulled back to sea from you, the earth moves slower. I am not rock and metal, don't ping when hit. Sand sifts through your fingers and packs my wrinkles, earth with water. I can keep you in between my toes, even when I'm underwater.

Maybe if you were Jonah we could be together. I'd rather consume you than hold you in my toes like talons.

**Nothing But Peeling (or, addict)**

he prayed Hail Marys into his cross
climbed three handsome stairs
and melted into the last

peeled wires from celery
leaving nothing but
yellow core

asked for forgiveness,
mercy and light, as
his pus-filled heart
drained onto his shirt

leaving empty the
atrium, ventricle
Virgin Mary
silver cross

**Still Here**

Inside the dried sticks, in the empty hair follicles, in the land of dry dirt, sand, begging for rain and pulling weeds so dried they're rotted, not from wet but straw-like sipping so strong and long, the silence is unbearable. The dry persists—a stem longs for us to pluck it from its sadness, put in a vase, amber lights, no sign of green or blue.

But cacti flourish here, a different, heartier, less vulnerable flower, and it is heart-y, like my hearts, dripping from stems, piling on the ground, only to make more.

And, my first born, (but not his first), I still hear you days later, crying in the back seat, waiting to be covered with the willow branches, tickled by their leaves, till I can give you more or just something different, as I have nothing to give, yet, nothing to hold.

The church windows stare, emotionless, and I hope there is some hymn he heard, as he flew from his bed and circled before leaving— because we are still here.

**Needmore Road**

You peer into darkness
listening to river sounds;
"It's really high tonight,
way over the banks."

But you keep staring at it
until the sun comes up,
like it's gonna go away

talking about the tree
that used to be over there
growing above the water, and
how you climbed it.

About walking through the river,
about being there with
Michael and Holly

and how this mountain laurel,
(you point), and that rhododendron
and that kudzu weren't there before.

You tell me how you signed a petition
to keep them from paving the road
next to this river.

And how you rode bikes 6 miles
down this road with your neighbor.

How you want to stay here,
get so drunk you
sleep in a hollow log.

**We Could**

She, only 3, said, "We could get him from up there."
Then she drew a map of scribbles, asked if we had a rope,
and planned just how we'd do it.

So we swung out over the earth with a swish of her fingertip,
grabbed her Daddy from heaven, and back over streams,
valleys, trees and over our neighbor's house, we brought
him home.

**The heart** holds the limbs in place.  Blood makes us upright.  The atrium is filled with color, light, the ventricle with the oil of thirty-three summers, and my hips sway from all of them.  There is something perfect in our valves, the opening of ourselves to blood and the closing of ourselves in pain.

Synapses, like fingers in surgery, touch our hearts.  Communication is lost somewhere in these gaps.  Between tire biting and blood loss, our hearts have teeth.

There's a song in our thumps
sometimes an old-time tune
sometimes a rap sometimes
a hummph, sometimes
a waiiil.

Our hearts stop at the most inappropriate times—choking on a new thought.

We are slaves.  People speak of passion as though it is something imprinted or burned
braised into our hearts, but as a matter of fact, it leaves through valves as quickly as it enters.

**on your birthday**

**(One).** I would swallow my heart
today if I could-
be your best friend

and make you a strawberry cake
or a chess pie

sing

light your candles
watch you make a wish
(not about me of course)
and blow them out

your lips would be pursed
as you blew
I'd watch

you'd have a piece of cake in one hand
a glass of whiskey in the other

the lines on your face
would get soft with a grin
and your shoulders would rise

and fall as you'd make
those noises you can't help making
when you laugh

spontaneous sounds
a crescendo then a decrescendo
part of your symphony that has always
bewitched me

**(Two).** today (on your birthday)
I almost ran off the road looking at
blackbirds flying in a V formation

we were in the blank space
you in the corner of the V
me at the opening

**speaking of swallowing my heart**

When I try to bite down,
it's all pink
and spittle
and lip.
(Tough to do with no teeth)

Anyway, hearts don't belong
in our bellies, slowly
digested in acid.
Veins would get tangled
traveling
switchback intestines.
We couldn't find ropes
or an oxygen line
leading back to the boat
or the balloon strings
we hold so tightly
(delighted with the floating)
if our hearts were digested.
We'd get lost with the anchor,
forget our dearest aches,
and the worst-

we'd shit out
the remains, and
waste the heart.

**Omen**

I can't drink the wine
My mouth is an extraordinary
Space
We think, probe red

I bare my throat to you
You laugh a song so selfish
I don't feel my flesh—
My eyebrows search for God

## Chapter 2: Feet to Water

**Raw Honey**

In folds of my skin

my fingers explore
your comb—

i taste you, soft

walk through a hall
made of beeswax, a smell
that will last for decades

hurt all the way to my fingertips

pollen
in 3 white rooms
bright piles
sunflower, dandelion, milkweed,

your face in my mind

and the st-ick sti-ck s-t-i-cky
stays
until hot water rinses
or it turns (in the cold) to a
heavy sugar

**a 27**

In the heart of my

dandelion

a century of

butterflies curl.

My pants ripping,

the wings unfold there.

**Stale Stick**

Don't lip me like an old cigarette.
I'll pull you into my feet
and spit you out of my brain.

**late**
in the afternoon
when things begin to calcify

I sit under the ceiling fan, blinking
at the light bulbs
and my eyes harden

it took 3 days for me to breathe you out
wear my shirt right side up again

milk pools in the middle of the saucer
laundry aches on the floor

the cat begs to go out
and I toss him out the door

heat and summer sun linger
like sweat on my neck
like your kiss—
then disappear

**on a full moon**

1.
i can see your face more clearly

the parts i don't want to see

that make this hole, the size of the

full moon

even more obvious

2.
in my yellow room, paper lanterns

on the floor

my chest toward the full moon

i open my ribs to let my heart

out

3.
i am hoping my heart will

leave

merge with the full moon

4.
make it new

**fruit**
is heavy on the trees
peaches touch the ground
branches curve

plums gather in purple masses
on the ground, bleeding
a rotten crop

she takes towels to bed
to keep blood from getting
in the sheets

but when something ripens
that heavy
it will bleed

**Taxonomy** (or the history of Christianity)

takes its place alongside the Mother Mary
She wants to hold the written word, Jesus, but they tear at her skirts.  They rock in her rocking chair writing formulas.

She eats placenta for nourishment.

Literacy gives men a chance to breathe superior.  They hallucinate on holy texts and laws.

She never survives Protestantism.
He is Collared and Christened.

She is displayed on a large stick of fire.
He reads stories of witches to his son.
Daughters play out these stories at night.

Some read holy texts just enough to fuck us up. They have taken away our Mother Mary, made her into a statue.

**Roundhouse**

kick to the chest
"BLAH BLAH" written in
stone on his grave

they buried him in a
sleeping bag
stuck him in the dirt

when he was alive
he drank warm whiskey-
a shot before every
road trip

honky tonk
bars on his breath
wild women gathered
around his handsome lips

he cracked open
hearts all over the place
till finally


he pissed off the wrong barmaid

**Kiss My Grits**

or the closest
bowl of mush you can find.

Tongue the tiny hominy
ground— buttered and
warm,

and when you finish
wipe your slobber
from the side of the bowl.

**Don't Make Me Do It**

I want to take your face
and smoosh it up
like putty, soft clay

watch your features change
listen to the splotch of
gums against teeth

lips touching nose
breath becomes a whistle.

I want to twist your earlobes
pinch your cheeks till they're
purple.

Bite your lips till they
bleed.

If you have any sense at all,
listen
and don't say a word.

**love song for lovers who can't be in love**

raking the yard, dried maple leaves
sun hiding behind closed gates
opening, we were gone

pulling out weeds by the roots
(the worst weeds grow upside down in us)

dancing alone, together
arms barely missing

pushing each other on the swing
until we pinch our hands
in the chains

## bound, or, I feel like a horny Emily Dickinson

bound feet and bound wrists,
bound to a story of lust
carnal birds flying wet wind

bound to a story of love
blue rain from brown eyes

beyond this place of yard-gnomes and wooden faces
planters on the porch and blackberry brambles in the
backyard

pretty meditations of starry places
where I can fly around the moon, and
there are none of my boundaries
(they are mine alone)

invisible as they are, they still exist
like lines drawn between dark and light

like when the noise stops

I am bound to my bedroom,
pale green walls and bookshelves
a soft blue chair,
paper lamps
my fences
and those words,

that do nothing they do nothing
in my head they do nothing—
on the page they do little else
but run around in the circles of o's

but I won't leave the yard
where blackberries stain my hands
and boundaries are easy freedom.

**Chapter 3: The Art of Dreaming**

**the art of dreaming**

all day has looked like evening
like it's perpetually getting ready
for dark

black blocks
will be placed
by men on ladders
over lingering bits of light
until the sky is
totally inky

then we ride up on the moon
and as we dream, we
take our place among
constellations

other living rooms play
our own in dreams
other people play
the ones we know, and

the images here are familiar
in an unfamiliar sort of way
draperies open to reveal
our selves

we slide down stairwells
on pillows
curtains close and
only our feet stick out

we can conjure ghosts
from the stained-glass ceiling

the paintings on the wall
change shape and color

when we ask

we walk into a house that
from the outside has only 3 levels
and climb 12 stories of stairs once inside, and
at daybreak we emerge
disoriented                                      wondering why we can't
fly anymore

**Immortals**

We hear grandfather clocks
chime on eons, and
take liberties with time
elongate days and pinch nights
in the ass smiling nicely
in circles and lines, hands
drip of hours, faces
of generations.

Today, we ride a second
hand. Tomorrow
the pendulum jerks, a piece
of creation severs. We sway
in time to the tides.

We're not lost here
in the ocean of mortals,
where fish drown in the sea.
We transcend the ancient idea, time.
Those damn fools the astronomers
thought they could measure us
with the gauge of orbs.
Please.
Mothers and planets know better.
We transcend the fabric of
home, hole, haven, and heaven.

**You'll recognize me**

I'm the angel
with fire coming out of my hands.

**Scarecrow**

I am infested with words, my life force a raven's breast. Crows in my field, I live with wheat and my feet dangle.

Lightning bugs show me earth.

Fabric covers me with skin.

I am a braid weaver.

I drink dust and rain, put my hands into the wind, alfalfa bites my neck, and

I push my hair back into my scalp.

**There's something wrong with me.**

I see your organs and the organ is playing and light is coming from the pipes, and the sound is bigger than my little eyes and my minuscule ears that hear pain in the midst of joy and joy in the midst of pain and God singing through the splintered trees and yellow air. It's all green and sickly and painful, and God hums a light song in the midst of it, and the lumps in her breast and the colors in the sky change and wind is curling spinning angry shifting and I wait for a new light from the pipes of this blistered tired struggling angry me-wait for shining newness, like Izzy, like Israel, like God Prevails.

**When we run,** we are going toward Light, and not toward each other
but parallel.  You know things I am only learning.  You run with me anyway.


She said, "When you see someone running next to you, then you'll know."

And as we run, the Light gets stronger.  We bend to It.  It wraps us,
vines around fragile, fearful hearts—fruitful, blooming, branching to Light.

**July 4th**
floating on our backs
following the flight
of the dragonfly

soft eyes
back and forth

too much homemade ice cream
in our bellies

we dance until we almost
puke, and twirl on the tile
on our butts

we want to be free of something
the heavy
pressing
darkness

so we light things on fire
and laugh at ourselves

**Playing at Religion**

Adults can watch people playing God
for only eight dollars a day,

makeshift crosses in their windows.

There are no more reasons to go home.

Come on through the turnstile
while they ignore you.

They play several rooms at once.

Infiniti balls will roll across the floor.

## Shadow, Our Puppet

We don't doubt this
opacity comes from us,
this authority to say
we are who we think we are.

Our shadow theatre on bricks
lengthened in the evening light.

We played in front of the wall,
making ourselves larger
or smaller at will.

My daughter asked why we
couldn't see our mouths.

We laugh at our strange ability
To control our dark
without hurting ourselves.
We master the shadows
connected to our feet.

The day she discovered her shadow,
she cried, afraid of its odd dancing
as she tried to run from it.

On the concrete
at noon, she was told she
should not see her shadow,
though she could.

Because she wasn't halfway between
the tropics, Cancer and Capricorn
she thought she was broken,
but she was seamless.

**Ripping**
roaring and fucking tearing the sheets
apart,
I jump out of the bed

in which I have almost lived
for weeks on end
entangling myself more and more
in the covers
reading, folding laundry,

looking out at the world through
palm leaves
writing, sleeping, dreaming,
letting the violin sounds take hold.

I have been off him for a full week now,
and there are limbs growing
out of my eyes and ears and mouth
that are about to bud.

The fences around me begin to teeter and rot
so I make paper from them
and I cut and fold myself into
tinier mes, then get frustrated
balling us up,
tying us in knots,
and then try to fix us.

Disentangled paper dolls
still crumpled,
but hang once again
overhead

like the ripped sheets,
now tacked to, cascading from
the ceiling.
I walk through them with my arms open.

I design a garden here,
in this new place-
(out of the bed, into the dirt)
planting myself
so my branches will keep growing,

and I go back to the beginning
back to the all
back to God.

**first day**

This is the day that the lawn
begins to grow,

and already she can't find herself
in the grass.

Corn grows quickly
in her field.

Her cotton bolls open, hands
reveal white puffs.

Her s e e d s erupt.
She finds sun, drinks water,

grabs soil, root-fingers
dirt deep under nails.

This is not slow-motion.
It's the swift burst of life.

## Cold Cut Generation

We are whooping it up
around here, like a nursing
home on Lawrence Welk night.

We know how to have a good time:
big hair, bright suits, matching makeup
and gospel choir for a full hour.

We shake our groove things and
laugh at ourselves, knowing how we look.

When it's time for Antiques Road Show,
we all wind down, and when the yard guy comes in, we are a bit
embarrassed.

We're not that old;
it's just that sometimes we have to stop watching the bad news,

Living it too.

Sometimes we have to dance with the baby.
Sometimes we just have to laugh at the funny outfits and the cheesy music.
Sometimes it's better to live the strange, the obtuse.

**Pollination**

I fly into the tops of trees, my horses half-hitched, hooves kicking pollen in my eyes. I can't control the sway of wildflowers, sit on hard, seedy middles, and sunflower seeds prick.

I pulled you out of my skin, plucked you like eyebrows grown wild. I could never hold a bloom that big in my hand, so I let it spill into my throat, swallowed it so hard no fingers could choke it up. Petals caress my ankles now. I pray for new seed.

**my bowl**

when I pray I push the clouds
aside
stand on my tiptoes, reach with both hands

sometimes I scoop out holes
or hack at them with scissors or
gardening shears

there's a bowl up there, ceramic
glazed robin's-egg blue
deep, thick sides
I'm beginning to fill

grabbing at balloon
strings
teetering atop a tall ladder—

when I've made a few holes
in the skyscape
and the bowl is heavy with prayer

I'll begin to sing louder,
stretch further on the axis
play with feathers in water
lift boulders with my pinkies

dive into the bowl
swim with my prayers
cut a cross-section, and
realize I've been heard.

**to build death**

She took ten pounds of red clay and slung it over her back, put some on her head for good measure. We think death is sharp, but she rounded the edges of a soft metal and took apart her concept of love, allowed it to wallow for a while, like her body floating in open water, ready for fish-nibbling,

and taxidermy crossed her mind
numerous times
but she couldn't get the image
of glass eyes out of her head,

so she ran naked in small circles around her trampoline, parts bouncing haphazardly, as if not actually attached.

Then she began to understand death: like layers of skin or guts
turned inside out and upside down, but not painful, only colorful and bright,
like the pink of a duodenum,

and she drowned in yesterday's bathwater, but it never got cold,
and she lived with beautiful death for the rest of her days.

**Prayer Room Floor**

this is the beginning, again— always beginning never ending, life to life, cupcakes fall, icing melts— we stand in the midst of the melting, the severing.
hands up, knees on pebble beds, in dirt  transformation, the rounding,
and all the angels float nearby.

we are covered by wings, circling, twisted gnarled, thorny sticks pierce perfectly, make holes for new skin.

where we begin is exhaustion, not where we end.

tumbleweeds, tornadoes, dust storms, half circles carved into the floor:  such reminders are Grace, sweeping away all the partial petals—littering curves of bodies, some dead, some sleeping.  this is the beginning
again.

**Morning Star**

Let me be your wet sand, and I will not fear,
but take your word and use it.
You let me dash myself in pieces
over and over.
Pick me up again, again.

I gave her to you at the altar,
but I have to stay close
until she can leave
without me dying too.

Your eyes blaze, burnished feet bear my weight.
I thank you weakly.

I'm more soapstone than iron,
and sharpening easily peels my layers.
I wear your stole,
precarious
on your altar.
Cathedrals rise, and spires jut into the clouds.

I sit among them in my nest,
frayed sticks
plucked down.

Oh Hosanna, You carry me
Grace, oh
Grace, oh
Grace in the river

## Author Biography

*Feet to Water* is Holly Dunlap's first book of poetry. She lives in the half-river, half-city of Florence, Alabama, with her daughter and her mother. She has a master's degree in creative writing from the University of Colorado, Boulder, and a bachelor's degree in English from Auburn University. Her poems have been published in journals including *The Denver Syntax*, *BlazeVox* in New York, and *Illuminations* at the College of Charleston, South Carolina.

"Her poems absorb and explore the world through as many dimensions as her experience has reached – in motherhood and loss, plants and planets, play, fear, lust, grief, God, numbness, love, and awe."

– Rebecca Massey

www.ingramcontent.com/pod-product-compliance
Lightning Source LLC
Chambersburg PA
CBHW060502110426
42738CB00055B/2594